TLACUILX: TONGUES IN QUARANTINE

Poetry by Project 1521

edited by
Yago S. Cura
Darren J. de Leon
Adolfo Guzman-Lopez
Linda Ravenswood de Montaño

Los Angeles | Hinchas de Poesía Press

Title: Tlacuilx: Tongues In Quarantine : poems, edited by Cura, Yago, de Leon, Darren J., Guzman-Lopez, Adolfo and Ravenswood de Montaño, Linda
Description: First Edition.
Los Angeles: Hinchas de Poesía Press (2021).

Copyright © 2021 by Hinchas de Poesía Press.
All rights reserved.
Printed in the United States of America

ISBN: 978-1-954640-90-0

Cover Design: Rainbow Underhill
Cover art: Sandy Rodriguez, Mapa de los Child Detention Centers Family Separations and other Atrocities, Hand Processed watercolor on amate paper, Collection of the artist. 94 1/2 x 47 in . Image: J6 Creative. © 2018 Sandy Rodriguez
Book Design: Autumn Anglin, GreyGirlGraphics.com

Requests for permission to reproduce material from this work should be sent to Hinchas de Poesía Press at yagoscura@gmail.com.

Project 1521: Cura, Yago (Editor)
de Leon, Darren J. (Editor)
Guzman-Lopez, Adolfo (Editor)
Ravenswood de Montaño, Linda (Editor)
Alvarez, Gloria Enedina (author)
Arancibia, Adrian (author)
Harris, Sara (author)
Iknadossian, Arminé (author)
Magaloni, Diana (author)
Rodriguez, Sandy (artist)

ISBN: 978-1-954640-90-0

TLACUILX: TONGUES IN QUARANTINE

Poetry by Project 1521

CONTENTS

FOREWORD 7
Luis J. Rodriguez

INTRODUCTION 11
Adolfo Guzman-Lopez

MARIPOSAS Y NIÑOS 16

17 | Detail of *Mapa de los Child Detention Centers and Family Separation and Other Atrocities*
Sandy Rodriguez

18 | For Pain in the Heart: Recipe
Arminé Iknadossian

19 | Faces On Amate
Adolfo Guzman-Lopez

interstitial: Sara Harris

22 | orchid bulb//fox blood//seafoam — a poultice
Linda Ravenswood de Montaño

interstitial: gloria enedina alvarez

25 | nonochton
Adrian Arancibia

27 | Imagínate
Yago S. Cura

29 | Dear little one/ Canto de Peces
Diana Magaloni

31 | Border Jamming
Darren J. de Leon

33 | The Artist Grows Wings
Arminé Iknadossian

34 | a golden sensation
gloria enedina alvarez

QUARANTINED TONGUES 36

37 | Detail of *Mapa de los Child Detention Centers and Family Separation and Other Atrocities*
Sandy Rodriguez

38 | Black Box
Adolfo Guzman-Lopez

40 | Oda a Antonio Valeriano
Diana Magaloni

42 | Life, From a Distance
Sara Harris

43 | Declare Peace Everyday
Sara Harris

45 | Elevation
Linda Ravenswood de Montaño

50 | Cae La Hojita
Adrian Arancibia

interstitial: Linda Ravenswood de Montaño

55 | Tlacuilos
Yago S. Cura

interstitial: Yago S. Cura

CONQUEST & RESISTANCE 60

61 | Detail of *Calavera Copters*
Sandy Rodriguez

62 | 1532
Adrian Arancibia

65 | 24 Karat
Adolfo Guzman-Lopez

interstitial: Arminé Iknadossian

68 | mirror of your eyes unseen
gloria enedina alvarez

69 | Calaveracopteros
Yago S. Cura

70 | The White Leather Bracelet
Darren J. de Leon

71 | Tiles, Scans, and Strong Feet
Darren J. de Leon

ANCESTOR BODIES 72

73 | Detail of *Mapa de los Child Detention Centers and Family Separation and Other Atrocities*
Sandy Rodriguez

74 | new moon
gloria enedina alvarez

75 | the body pulse
gloria enedina alvarez

interstitial: Darren J. de Leon

78 | ENTRE Y CUANDO
gloria enedina alvarez

79 | Between When at Times
gloria enedina alvarez

80 | Julia Bogany on empowering the future

WRITER'S BIOS 82

ACKNOWLEDGEMENTS 85

ABOUT PROJECT 1521 86

FOREWORD

Poetry and the American Holocaust:
Generating beauty and truth to confront the ugly and the lies

Luis J. Rodriguez

In your hands is poetry emanating from a deeply disturbing "original sin"—the conquest and domination of Mexico, Central America, and what we call Latin America.

Can verse unveil and redeem such ruin? Can it guide us to re-imagine ourselves on our long and blood-ridden journey to comprehensive human liberation and dignity?

I believe in poetry. Poets and writers from the United States, Mexico, Guatemala, El Salvador, Honduras, Nicaragua, Chile, and other countries have long proven the power of imagery, language, and story to do exactly that. Today, we need poetry more than ever. But it's important for me to provide a remarkable and expanded context for such shaping.

We are still anchored to this horrific past even as we open space for brave and abundant conceptions of what should be in the present and future, here and everywhere. One of the most momentous clashes of cultures that shaped the whole world, not just a country or a landmass, but the whole freaking planet, in ways it could never return from, and from which new worlds had to be born, was when Spain began its conquest and colonial domination of the so-called New World with the "big bang" sparked by the 1492 voyage of Christopher Columbus. Starting a year after, Papal Bulls issued by popes Nicholas V and Alexander IV enshrined "The Doctrine of Discovery" in almost all laws of the land for the control by the Spanish, Portuguese, Dutch, English, and French. Any non-Christian peoples were designated as not human. The lands they lived on and cultivated were considered "vacant" and could be taken and owned by Europeans. The "pagans" and "heathens" could be enslaved. For 400 years or so these imperial relationships lasted until countries newly formed from the morass began their wars of independence, and largely hybrid peoples emerged to rule.

The first thing Spain, et al, had to do was create a wholly fabricated concept of race superiority and a history-wide justification for some of the worst atrocities, theft, and destruction one set of human beings ever did to another. Of course, this clash—not an "encounter" or "adventure" but a total usurpation of life, culture, economies, and peoples—also enveloped Africa, with millions of its inhabitants brought to this subjugated world called *Las Americas* (North, Central, and South America as well as the Caribbean).

This devastation turned out to be a holocaust, a word of Greek origin that drew from an older Hebrew word. For the Greeks it meant "burnt offering" to appease whatever Gods demanded such sacrifices. For the power and well-being of the few, others had to be trampled on and destroyed. That's holocaust.

The accumulation of wealth that had been derived from free land, free labor, free silver & gold & diamonds, and later oil and other minerals, also fueled the development of the northern hemispheric capitalist system. This soon extended to people and lands in the Mideast, South Asia, Asia, the Pacific islands, and "down under." As the British loved to say, its flag never set within the vast expanse of its empire. This is true, again, for any European power that benefited directly from such domination (many European countries never took part in such events, but indirectly benefited from the relative opulence these fortunes wrought).

A key historical turning point proved to be Hernan Cortez's conquest of the Mexica (so-called Aztecs) that later enveloped the Mayan and other indigenous peoples of present-day Mexico and Central America. Anthropologists call this area Mesoamerica. It is considered one of seven "cradles of civilization" where writing, agriculture, architecture, technology, and more arose independently of any other. Although Mesoamerica arrived later than when the Niger River, Nile River, Tigris & Euphrates rivers, Yellow River, Indus Valley, and Andean civilizations first evolved, it did so in grand style. We have yet to unlock all its secrets. Thousands upon thousands of temples and other construction lie beneath jungles and water. Their complicated writing systems have only recently started to be deciphered. Mesoamerica's vast ancestral knowledge of nature and the cosmos has yet to be fully grasped.

With disease and massacres, using superior arms, horses, and harboring an insatiable drive for riches, within 50 years of Cortez's arrival an estimated 90 percent of the peoples of Mesoamerica disappeared. Some 25 million were believed living there with 2.5 million still standing following that period. One report claimed you could find your way to the newly constituted capital of "New Spain" (Mexico City today) by the smoke from indigenous people burning at the stake. At least 60,000 *amate* bark paper books were destroyed. Today only a handful of pre-conquest books exist. Most ancient codices—around 500—were created by *Tlacuilos* (painter-writers) during colonial times.

I am—being at least half indigenous through DNA—descended from the 10 percent who lasted, labored, intermarried, had children, and began to repopulate what we call Mexico and Central America. Yes, these countries are not fully indigenous. They have significant Spanish, other European, African, Asian, Mideastern, and more among its present-day peoples. But the vast pool of who we are, our profoundest root, is indigenous. There are still more than 20 million more-or-less traditional original peoples in Mexico and Central America. Even more in South America. Also, the vast number of indigenous peoples who have no more ties to their tribe, languages, or traditions. And, of course, the millions who have been transformed from ongoing *mestizaje* (mixing of peoples and cultures) that continues in Latin America, as well as the US regions they settled in.

Just the same, for me, I gravitate to my indigenous. My teachers and elders have come from among the Mexica of Mexico and the United States; the Rarámuri (Tarahumara of Chihuahua, Mexico); Dine (Navajo); Lakota; Akimel O'odham; Santee Sioux; Mayan (Mexico & Guatemala); Pibil (El Salvador); and Quechua (Peru).

One thing poetry should declare is the end of considering blood, mixing, and all other racial categorization that the Spanish brought with their *casta* (caste) system. We are not part this, part that; this "race" or that "race," this DNA and that DNA (my own DNA exploration notwithstanding). We are whole and complete as we are, whenever or however we were born. And from here, we must rethink and rebuild.

Poetry is a good place to start. A beacon on our mutual road to becoming fully human, fully caring, fully creative. No more children in cages! No more people, mostly indigenous, working and living under the shadow of unequal and undignified US immigration laws! No more discriminating against and dismissal of refugees from nation-states, again all fabricated concepts, suffering from extreme climate change, poverty, corruption, and violence!

Poetry, like all art, can illuminate our way as we implement the essence of our dreams into the essence of our realities. It is some of the most important truth and beauty we can muster to confront and challenge the systemic race-and-class foundations our countries were built on. We need new soil for the kind of generative garden we must now seed.

—Luis J. Rodriguez
Los Angeles, June 2021

INTRODUCTION

Adolfo Guzman-Lopez

In 2018 I was shaken by a painting of a cactus. It was made on paper made of bark and fiber. The color was like nothing I'd seen, but it was as familiar as the smell of wet earth when it rains. The color was made of a natural dye that made me jettison all the greens of my Mexican childhood — the flag, the political party emblems, el soldado in primary reading books, ribbons in braided hair, and even the Virgen de Guadalupe's shroud — as artificial, imposed. The land, this green was saying to me, is the true mother, the true source, and deserving of praise.

Painter Sandy Rodriguez had been creating her own natural paint dyes using indigenous methods. She had also begun a deep dive into the Florentine Codex, the 1570s document painted and written by indigenous artists, or tlacuilos. When I say deep, I mean deep. She bought a multi-volumen facsimile of the Codex. She painted on amate paper, which had been outlawed in Colonial New Spain.

The Florentine Codex depicted and described, in Spanish and Nahuatl, the dying and transforming cultural practices of a people in the first stage of a painful process of colonization. It would become an encyclopedic book born out of a time of crisis.

The 1570s artists and writers embedded into the codices the messages and ideas that depicted a world that was being destroyed and transformed, and the violence they'd endured with their parents and grandparents in the 50 years since the conquest in 1521.

Sandy's codices depicted our current time of crisis: environmental destruction, family separations, and unaddressed violence that is part of our environment as much as canyons, mesas, and coastlines.

Which brings me back to the cactus which prompted me to question the patriotism and nationalism that burst within me — a flor de piel — that in my teens and twenties I had attached to symbols. The cactus seemed to be saying that loyalty should be toward the land, the original provider, and that sustainable stewardship of the land is the true patriotism.

For decades I'd gathered voices against social injustice to form performance poetry groups and reading series, first with the Taco Shop Poets in 1994 in San Diego then the Spine of Califas reading series in Los Angeles in the early 2000s. Those projects became choirs of polyphonic voices writing testimonies. These were stories of painful migration, love that is transmitted generation after generation, and the corrosive nature of popular media, and many other topics.

The writers we invited to be part of Project 1521 were long-time poetry collaborators, veteran writing teachers and performers, pre-Columbian scholars, all from different cultural backgrounds. There is no one label to describe us. The meetings, workshops, chit chat, lunches, dinners, and readings brought us together. We began to hear each other's voices and found a common key in which to sing.

We met in Sandy's art studio, slightly more than a one-car garage, surrounded by her paintings and listened to her describe her trips to the backcountry in search of minerals and plants for her art. Diana Magaloni, the former director of the National Museum of Anthropology in Mexico, gave us master classes in Mesoamerican indigenous art and cosmology. We learned how there was meaning embedded in the use of colors made with plant or mineral dyes. We heard descriptions of the conditions the tlacuilos worked under as they put the last drops of ink on paper. A pandemic forced them to sequester near the end of their work.

The Project 1521 writers recognize we are on the cusp of a different world. It's not a foregone conclusion what that world will look and feel like. We believe in action to bring about acts of loving kindness and justice. Our ancestors' migration experiences had layovers in Lebanon, Argentina, Chile, Chihuahua, Chicago, Miami, San Francisco, National City, Guadalajara, Mexico City, and many points in between. Some of our ancestors' names are lost to us, like the names of those who died through the violence of colonialism after 1521. Recovering and keeping their names should be an ongoing process.

This idea came to me in 2018 during a family trip to Jerusalem. After entering Yad Vashem, Israel's Holocaust museum, I came across a display of a partly burned Torah scroll recovered from *kristallnacht*, the 1938 pogrom against Jews in Germany. It was more than a burnt page. The Torah scroll is a compendium of hyperlinks to spiritual healing, past, present, and future.

It shook me to see this holy book desecrated. What would have been the reaction of members of the congregation to which it belonged? It's the book read on Holy Days, and special occasions. On Bar and Bat Mitzvahs, it soaks up tears of joy and pain. So many voices that have given sound to it's words. That part of it went up in smoke and hit close to home. It hit close to my mestizo soul, my Mexican soul, my Catholic soul, my American soul, and the part of my soul that comes from the sparks of my wife and kids' Jewish souls.

Then I had a vision, a daydream in that low-lit gallery. I saw the indigenous texts of Tenochtitlan rise in embers above the Aztec capital, consumed as they rose higher, and falling, landing gently onto the bloody waters of the canals. I imagined a young woman, about the age of Moses' sister Miriam, lean over, pick up the pieces and gather them in a reed basket: a coffin of words.

There is a rotunda at Yad Vashem. It is a circular library with shelves nearly filled with notebooks that contain the names of the people murdered in the Holocaust. The books are not finished. There are still names to be added, information to be added and corrected.

What we've gone through in Project 1521 is hard to measure, because it's impossible to bottle and package the insights we have had listening to teachers and spending time in front of works of art. As we took stock of struggle, pain, and death in our own time and put it side by side to that of our ancestors, we saw that our contribution should have healing as its purpose. So we recover our ancestors' names, and more importantly, their experiences. The land has been the conduit of those conversations, it's been the hollowed-out canoe, the river we glide on, the tree under which we sit.

The writing in this book is our beginning, the opening bars to a long symphonic piece that is not linear and not quite circular, but multidimensional.

Thank you for listening.

Tongva Land Acknowledgement

We, the Indigenous People,
The Traditional Caretakers of this landscape are the direct descendants of the First People who formed our lands, our worlds, during creation time. We have always been here. Our ancestors prepared and became the landscapes and worlds for the coming of humans with order, knowledge, and gifts embedded in the landscape. Our Ancestors, imbued the responsibility and obligation to our original Instructions, guided by protocol and etiquette to be part of, take care of, and insure the welfare of the extended family and community defined in its most inclusive expression, the NATURE and to pass those teachings and responsibilities onto our children, grandchildren and many generations to come. (AND to all those that now live here).
- Awiskahe

For Julia Bogany (1948 - 2021)
We dedicate these poems to you and your energy that blessed us.

MARIPOSAS Y NIÑOS

Detail of *Mapa de los Child Detention Centers and Family Separation and Other Atrocities* by Sandy Rodriguez. Image: J6 Creative. Collection of the artist

For Pain in the Heart: Recipe

Arminé Iknadossian

- dedicated to 16-year-old Juan de León Gutiérrez, 7-year-old Jakelin Caal Maquin, 8-year-old Felipe Gómez Alonzo, 2-year-old Wilmer Josué Ramírez Vásquez, 16-year-old Carlos Hernandez Vasquez, 20-month-old girl Mariee Juárez, and 10-year-old Darlyn Cristabel Cordova-Valle who died in the custody of U.S. Customs and Border Protection

Take the juice of the nonochton azcapanyxua,
an herb that grows near ant hills.
Mix with gold leaf, resin from amber,
shavings from turquoise, red coral, ochre.

Kill a stag with your bare hands,
slice its chest open. Pull out the steaming heart
still beating. Start a fire with witch hazel and brush,
roast the stag heart till charred, burnt black.
Slice off a piece of the heart.

Mix all with water.
Sip the potion that tastes like soil,
shimmers like 24 karat starlight,
taste the blues and reds, the blood
and marrow of the sacrificial animal.

The red ants crawling through
your ventricles will disappear.
Then your chest will open,
your fists will unclench,
and your hands will transform into desert flowers.

Faces On Amate

Adolfo Guzman-Lopez

Felipe of the year of my Elyanna.
Felipe of the year we became tlacuilos,
the year our fists unclenched into words.

Protesto,
the eyes among the fibers
are the layers of earth.

Protesto,
each child wears
a badge of quetzal.

Protesto,
the fibers run up
to their faces,
the edges of the hills.

Protesto,
America is
a scar on Felipe's cheek.

And Jakelin, and Mariee, and
Darlynn, and Carlos, and Juan.

In total time
I will understand
how your heart stopped beating.

In total time
I will understand
how we allowed
our cities to be toppled,
our souls taken
hostage faraway.

In total time
we will meet.

You teach me your song,
our breaths a choir
harmonize the prayer of peace,
you for me
and me for you.

interstitial: Sara Harris

    To hold in my mind the portraits of the children lost in the same space as las diosas que protejían a sus jornadas al retorno; this has kept my sense of honor, privilege, and responsibility in common and in check, as a mother, during these times of La Pandemia y las injusticias fronterizas.

orchid bulb//fox blood//seafoam — a poultice

Linda Ravenswood de Montaño

For 7 children who perished in U.S. ICE detention, 2019

Darlyn Cristabel Cordova-Valle
Jakelin Caal Maquín
Felipe Gomez Alonzo
Juan de Leon Gutiérrez
Wilmer Josué Ramírez Vásquez
Carlos Hernandez Vásquez
Mariee Juarez

You will not be forgotten
nor ever
   though you return
to air and earth
you will be in the dawn again —
braided in our bread —

     our ox bones will bear the need of you
     the essential you

our leaves and trees will increase with you
we will imbibe of you
(our riverwater will increase
because of you).

   We will imbibe of you in night.
    — you the remanded
    the terrorized   the swept
    you   the medicine for our children

     though no star shattered to feed you
     in the tremor
     in your hour of need

your mother's hands // a fury

Mariposas y Niños

// a cloud // all fastness // to bring you over //
the eternal recurrence of your gift //
your footprint   your Smallfoot
   on the place // every desert
plant and eye will become you
   you will not be forgotten // you
your useful voice will sing in the desert again
your *childcall* and *ghostwisdom*
your strength to withstand conquest
an ancient battalion
against bronze heavy hands
a pressure sacrilegious from outside you

— your strength to rebuild
the tower of our people
over and again — your ironweed —
your night — your time under glass —

   though your throat was closed
it will be the tributary —
   the medicine of your veins
will speak the healing

— your body will return the protection
   of which you were robbed

   your body the breakers
   your body the rock
   your body the breath
   your body the night
   your body the safety
   your body the light
   your body the tunnel of grass
   your body the place
   your body our coven
   your body our wood

      — until you become everything

interstitial: gloria enedina alvarez

Constantly traversing the city, I find inspiration in its many cruces, crossings, and portals. Like its roads and intersections, my work alone, collaboratively, and in community, maps the migrations and transmigrations of memory and place, drawing on my own and my family's experience of repatriation and interior exile. The concept of Nepantla, a consequence of historical events beginning with colonization, is once again addressed through the collaboration with Project 1521, as we, like our ancestors, face a pandemic. It invokes the fragmentation of the self in that state of either/or, ni aquí, ni allá, by establishing a dialogue that evolves to a fluid aquí y allá, both here and there, present as a whole, as a person and as a people. Images of the healer and of the children who died in detention camps by Sandy Rodriguez call out to the ancestors, call out to us, cara, corazón y manos, face, heart and hands.

nonochton

Adrian Arancibia

en mi pecho
estás tu.
seno, leche
que el llanto suelta
leche que cura
la respiracíon
leche.

y que pasa
a los hijos e hijas
que están
apartados de sus padres
cuáles llantos
corren como leche
y sin leche?
llantos, pero qué llantos?
cuántos padres
que no serán padres
de hijas e hijos.

esa ausencia
no hemos sentido
desde cuando...

and it hurts
to heal. to feel
the estrangement
extrañar
lo que no está
ya.
como ver la cara
entre rostros.
face among faces.
in between senos.
where the christ child should
have been.

that child,
hijo del hombre
daughter of woman
silence.

we love
because they
are in hearts
in chests
pounding.

giving life.
giving until
they have no life to give.
and it hurts
to know there will
be no more cries.
no more words
to create rivers.
to create milk.
and sustenance
for humanity.

Imagínate

Yago S. Cura

Imagine making
Arizona from Guatemala
on foot, on thousands of feet.

Imagine getting nicked by the
security apparatus of a dying,
belligerent country.

Imagine your only solution is breach
barbed wire river-borders, sea chasms
or death valleys.

Imagine you save a fortune
to pay a stranger in a long line of strangers
and there's no guarantee any
of them aren't charlatanczars.

Imagine your parents receive video
of you on the other side of some miserable,
invisible line as some sort of trafficking receipt.

Imagine the middle of the desert,
thick with theodolites from all the angles
spent ingressing, spent coalescing
a horizontal or vertical entry plane.

Imagine the milky hulls of half-empty jugs
abandoned in the scrub like cairns or hollow
teeth dedicated to Thirst.

Imagine going from evaporated-milk-
stars and black-coffee-skies to constellations
of ducts and closed-circuit-scalpel-cameras.

Imagine you hoard all the flu shots, all the ridiculous
bars of soap, all the too-tiny-toothbrushes, all the instant
coffee and creamer packets, all the jailhouse slippers

and super sad-ass uniforms, all the indigent kits,
all the stainless steel toilets and basins,
all the toddlerpods and bargain panopticons
that you can sardine into a convention center.

Imagine. you convert a Walmart
into a concentration camp,
a supermarket into a Tribunal of Sand,
a presidency into a jingoistic gangland
rampart ampere hellbent on mutiny.

Imagine someone, somewhere,
in some fake-ass fatherland board
room asking something integral
to the conversation, something, like,
like on what aisle, and at what height
should we fly our federally-mandated,
yet, shiny-as-fuck defibrillators?

Dear little one/ Canto de Peces

Diana Magaloni

Los Angeles, March, 22, 2019

Dear little one,
you took it upon yourself to carry
the burden of our destiny.

You screamed your lungs out
with courage,
as you were burnt
by an unfathomable blaze.

As night dawned,
Midnight turned into midday
you were turned into fish,
to swim across
the cold, murky, waters
of lake Texcoco,
filled with blood and human flesh.

This is the task
you took upon your shoulders
To be fish and carry the sun.
To be fish and worship a new god.
To be fish and plow the earth,
with flowers.
To be fish and spread
the ancestral seeds of our future.

Like fish,
you are prey of the greedy
Like fish,
you are ignored and consumed.

But you continued swimming,
together,
like fish.

To cleared the water,
To turn it
into the crystalline living substance
that sustains us

Like water,
You are eighty percent
of our blood.
Like water,
Your death
meant our creation.

Border Jamming

Darren J. de Leon

Tonight, they stabbed all of my wounds
and poured gasoline over my head.
And who are you?
Funky multi-national caravan
walking in the thousands
Bluetooth cumbia wireless headset

Entonces, un chamaco de Oaxaca,
sister raped in the belly of the jeep.
He cries in sleepless tears.
Now he knows Narco kindness,
smack, cocaine, hepatitis,
as a body's slashed head-to-toe.

The machine gun in the closet
the nightmare of empty eyes (in a border jam)
the safety of a crossing
blistered feet, still he rise. (in a border jam)
In earthquakes and wasted rivers
facebook spreads like bees (in a border jam)
The Utah Jazz are crystal white
Salt Lake City chopped at the knees (in a border jam)

Smuggling is what smugglers smuggle.
Billionaires upon the hill
can slide their nose across the mirror.
Wearing red hats of hate and torched ignorance
Once inside, the executive is frightened
of diners and backfires.

Now guerillas fight for freedom
Vultures use the stacked courts (in a border jam)
Snakes cage up the babies
in chain link prison forts (in a border jam)
While inside hieleras
below where two countries meet
The seekers grab at plastic bags

filled with food to eat
america lacks empathy and kindness
it's intentional, too! (in a border jam)

Now shaky ports of entries claim
a thirst for the oil of Venezuela.
The twitter feed is abuzz
with pictures of mi abuela.
I thought I saw Iris Chacon!
Compas y Hermanas!
Iris Chacon!
In a border jam!
Aw, now that is the movida
I gotta see!

Undocumented and proud of it!

The Artist Grows Wings

for Sandy Rodriguez

Arminé Iknadossian

She is doing something illegal, laying her sleeping bag
somewhere she shouldn't. She lays down
with her back to the moon, watches the mountains

made of red rocks, every minute, a new shadow,
a sharp cut of light, magic like sore feet and dusty backpacks,
magic like a young girl floating behind a mother
who holds tight the child's hand - a ribbon tied to a balloon

in the shape of a small girl.
This is California. Arizona. Texas.
This is not a yellow street sign on the highway north of Baja,
not factory-made, not municipal, not paid for by taxes.

The image is a movie on the face of the red rocks,
it is every mother and child running.
Running so fast, the girl grows wings, takes off.
She is red, she is brown, she is sky.

a golden sensation

gloria enedina alvarez

nostalgia's precise memory no longer enduring and inescapable...

yet profound and courageous...

accurate as death...

QUARANTINED TONGUES

Detail of *Mapa de los Child Detention Centers and Family Separation and Other Atrocities* by Sandy Rodriguez, Photo credit: J6 Creative. Collection of the artist

Black Box

Adolfo Guzman-Lopez

Tlacuilos worked the materials like clay, stone, and wood. They picked up the splinters and shards of their grandparents' world, sequestered, building a universe that would later be called the Florentine Codex by people with faraway cataract telescopes.
They sheltered in place, a hole in the wall let in an image of the outside world.
Upside down, the outside world makes sense.
Our room is Sandy's studio, a converted one car garage in Mar Vista. It's the part of the city smoothed by thousands of years of morning marine layers that ground the rich soil.
We keep the morning marine layer in our lungs as long as we can. We exhale.

Adrian witnesses
Adolfo witnesses
Arminé witnesses
Darren witnesses
Diana witnesses
Gloria witnesses
Leticia witnesses
Linda witnesses
Julia witnesses
Sara witnesses
Yago witnesses

We look at each other. The crisis of the truth leads us to question, leads us to wonder whether words have power, leads us to realize words have power.
Words lift the dead from burial, make the sun rise. Words allow us to see the tlacuilos in their harvest shelters of volcanic rock.
They write, they paint, they choose the ink. Sometimes it's red, sometimes it's black, made of stone, made of roots, made of petals light enough to be taken by the wind and dropped on the channels that are no longer there. The channels choked by concrete to the sea.
Temple stones piled,
the sickness,
mothers dead,

the decoders
of the dreams dead.

Obsidian and steel.
When we close our eyes we are in total time, surrounded by black
stone walls, porous enough for us to hear what's going on outside
but sharp enough to bleed our fingerprints if we escape.
Outside, the world falls apart. Within these black walls we
remember to create an image that is not a representation, but it's
own universe.
We never lived in a world without toppled temples,
we never lived in a world without embers and the smell of burned
amate. The drumming, the beat, the souls of our feet grinding soil,
wet and dry.
How do we keep the words from disappearing?
How do we keep the words from turning to dust?
The secret is in the flower.
Take the orchid, it's petals, it's smell.
And wrap the words, for us, our children, and the ancestors.
15191521160016501700175018101821191019171992199420192021

Oda a Antonio Valeriano

Diana Magaloni

22 de Marzo, 2019

Antonio Valeriano, sabio nahua, co-autor del Códice Florentino y gobernador de La República indígena de México en 1570. Se cree que es autor en náhuatl de la aparición de la Virgen de Guadalupe, llamada Nican Mopohua.

Te sientas en una estera de juncos,
Antonio Valeriano.

Los juncos que son el verdor de la tierra,
y tejidos
son toda tu gente: Nican titlaca. Los que somos aquí.
Antonio Valeriano.

Pero los juncos crecidos y multiplicados sobre el agua,
brillan en el sol claro de la mañana

Y erguidos así, luminosos, piensas:
son los rayos de un nuevo sol.

Los espíritus de todo lo que existe y tiene vida:
aves, peces, felinos, serpientes, lobos poderosos,
no hay fin.

Los juncos tejidos de tu estera,
Antonio Valeriano,
son el mundo en unidad

Que hoy como gobernador de México,
debes conducir con sabiduría.

Sentado en la estera de juncos
Antonio Valeriano,
tus pensamientos alcanzan
la más alta frecuencia

Son como los minerales de una roca

y las células de colores de las flores.

Tus pensamientos hacen al mundo.

Sentado sobre la estera de juncos,
Antonio Valeriano,
en un ahora de multiplicidad y expansión vertiginosa
del tiempo y el espacio.

Tejes nuevas palabras en náhuatl, español y latín
y haces aparecer la imagen de la nueva Madre Tierra.

Nos regalas a Tonanzin-Guadalupe,
sabiendo que su manto de estrellas
y vestido de flores,

seguirá teñido de sangre indígena
  por los próximos quinientos años

Life, From a Distance

Sara Harris

Some are compelled
>to document
>>every change
>>>every wonder
>>>>every moment

every movement that
>shapes the day.
>>Some already
>>>pulled away
>>>>from the clinging to

the wheel while
>Some fall
>>Some are thrown
>>>Some sit alone
>>>>on top
>>>>>to ponder

the Ground
>without ever touching it.

Declare Peace Everyday

Sara Harris

A Vow
    of silence
        amidst
            the violence
                Because
                    "Hate is
                        too heavy
                              a Burden..."

The water
    wise Garden
        awaits us all.
                A Vow
                    of silence
                        Because

The violence
    Hovers
        in the air.
            "Hate is
                too Heavy
                    a burden
                        to Bare."

"If a (wo)man
    has lost
        a relative
            (s)he is Forbidden
                to Engage
                    (in rage)
                        in Business
(as usual)
    Until
        Thirty Days
            after
                the death."
                    No Breath
                          if One of Us
                              can't breathe...

Reprieve
       is not
             an option
                  Because
                        the Fix is In:
                              We're here to begin
                                      when "Hate is
                                              too heavy
                                        a Burden."

Elevation

Linda Ravenswood de Montaño

Winter 2018
When I sign on
to the project
the 500 year anniversary
of the Mexican conquest
it seems important —
but of all its history
it's the navigations
in half and half
that keep calling
        For instance,
I remember being stunned
by *wetback* — my mother
is white
and my father
code switches
        from seafaring angles
        at all sides.
— those iterations
move along —
like they always do.

In winter
the project is important —
scratches at identity
the idea of dignity
        scratches like
           the softest / roughest / denuded
reaching branch
at the window

Summer 1521
Psychotically,
painfully relevant
      the monk
gathers
      20 Nahuatl scribes —
— smart boys — able boys —
          to write down everything
          — to listen at every color
          and band of leaf —
          every bend of marrowbone
          and piece of glass and gold
          in Vermilion Sea.
Through the windows of the college they watch
as families bend
      and disintegrate —
no one brings
even a cup of water —
      no help
        no hazmat suit
everything decimates —
heads once ordained
 ornamented
polished
 pressed
pigmented
 blessed
split open
like gourds
in the plaza —
they watch
from the windows —
it is relevant.

Summer 2021
I watch
from a window
built by swift Chinese —
push-button factory workers who
like the scribes of México
leave home to mark a new age —
anyone listening

Quarantined Tongues

I watch from windows
assembled / dissembled
by industry —
brought round the world
on the traffic of boats
    what is that house on the water
    coming

Summer 2021
One of my cousins has Covid.
COVID 19 — she is recovering.
(I tell no one
I think
I had Covid in February.
Covid is shameful
not being strong is shameful
vulnerable is shameful
I tell no one —
I give myself broth
and start to walk.
Even though I'm tired
I walk the quarantine house —
then outside — in circles
to build my cardiovascular —
I take vitamins
and try to rest —
at night I pray at vigil
that breath would return
    come back inside of me my breath
I buy an
oxygen meter — & watch —
one day
I think
I would have to go
to the hospital.
I sign the checks
and put on makeup.
But as I work
it begins to be very late —
so instead of going
I climb into bed
and little by little
I begin to feel better.)

Tell no one.

Summer 2021
I look through windows
phone and tablet —
ancient words — new mirrors
   that's why you have a big piece of property
   that's why you want acres
   so no one can come near you
we wonder — how did anyone ever leave their
house again — we scoffed at *chadur*
& the wearing of a veil —
covering up was unAmerican,
not French, *c'est impossible*,
& now — it is against the law
to go without our faces draped.
We think we know everything.
   The narcissism of now
   fills us with amnesia.
The headlines
have always been the same
but we don't know this
because we can't even
remember our mother's maiden name.

Summer 2021
Another cousin has Covid.
How could Covid
come to the
sleepy town
where my father was born.
Deep in Vermillion Ocean
marlins course red mercury water
marlines y tortugas y tiburones
— they ride close to shore
slow, leatherback turtles
shuttling blue dreams
in sand pits where my father was born.
I watch in windows
like the white half
the safe, Nahuatl 20 half
the know-what half

Quarantined Tongues

the now-what half
the Mayflower half
the 21st-century half
the 16th/20th-century scribe
an endless, gravitational pull of Cortes
— *this mirror revolves*

Summer 2021
My cousin is intubated.
His children have Covid.
His wife has Covid.
His mother is alone in her house with Covid.
La Paz, Baja California Sur, Mexico.
How is the plague relevant,
primo.

Summer 2021
My cousin's ashes were blessed in La Paz
live via Facebook.

Cae La Hojita

Adrian Arancibia

"Cae la hojita
Tan pequeña,
con sonrisa tan buena
Y de amanecida, en que te has convertido
Sueño de una flor, que linda creció
que nunca seco, tú eras la hojita que cayo."
La hojita - Tambobrass

I.

sometimes, the cold air feels
things seem exceedingly clear.
and it's cool. like tonight, i hear
the voices. the voices code switch.
'tween nahuatl & quechua.
& spanish overlaid by english.
the end of the line. waiting to be
understood by chileno/chicano.
on the ledge,
        on the edge,
                the border.
the love
        always
more complex. remembers.
the love.

looking. for omens.
for words.
certain eyes for
feathers. certain maps we keep
                we
trace on a wall.
we trace with an overhead.
        a projector.
still awaiting,
        translations,
                translitics.
still.

II.

hand holds pen.
hand works patience
worn bones. ache. aching.
tracing flor y canto.
& the closest i've seen:
los jaivas
on machu picchu.

voices, canto. words. but,
that morning didn't have words. only
sighs of sickness.
crypto-indigenismo.
following. the
storm, thundering. in chests.
even with categorizations:
species, genus, family.
        order to existence.
to a heart
still weeping. lives.
she weeps,
death, dying, dying in a lake. or snake.
where la llorona weeps.
where we cut, we spliced.
inglés/spanish/nahuatl/quiché/quechua
and yet, marti, bolivar, and vasconcelos
origin mythos.

and
language and death
    still
        mark.

III.

the scary thing.
500 years later,
scores ain't settled.
no tlaxcalan democracy been named.
no mapudungun toqui.
no chango map.

no aymará glyph.
just us.
                      swimming
        the discourse.
white meeting red.
           and atlantic black to pacific.

my family back in barros arana.
or better yet, calle bellavista.
in iquique, know.

the new battles named it
fredy taberna. or santa maria.
searching the routes.
marking the passages.

reading nahuatl versions of scripts.
codices as me these days.
and i'm looking for home.
and found nothing but,
betrayal and sickness.
and frankly, i'm not sure
which is worse.

IV.

now.
children in prisons.
love, thing of past.
children awaiting homes
they might never
            walk through.
the quiché say, time never stops

for these hearts,
                    it does.
like mapuche lonko hearts.
like mexica llorona tears.
hearts fed seeds.

hearts.
children hoping

for more. like flor y canto.
we can't separate the two.
'cause the poet says,
before music,
was the word. then,
the word,
with music. music begun
with a beating heart.

interstitial: Linda Ravenswood de Montaño

And yet, the urge to make the image goes on. We don't know for whom we are writing, or singing, or painting. It may only be for ourselves and the wind. Some subtle urgency between the animal and the mineral. Our breath and the ancient immovable earth.

Writing, thinking, and talking this way is like trying to decipher your father's moves. Your mother's intentions. Impossible!

Tlacuilos

Yago S. Cura

in Aztec glyphs
the symbol for painter:
two diagonal scrolls in a
rectangular frame.

in a Mar Vista garage-
taller: a modest lecture
hall on grinding cochineal
to make eon-old red;

in Nahuatl and chilango
slang, in lunfardo from Buenos
Aires and Spanglish from Los Angeles
in Lebanese Arabic and Maya
in Quechua and Zapotec.

in a Long Beach synagogue
or Pacoima tacoshop; in poetry brothels
constructed from bones of faith corporations,
in groves of spoiled fruit.

in training painters to be a class
of sonic illustrators in the calmecac;
in holding two to three part-times
in the hopes of adding up one vocation;
in attaining gifted witness status
as compilers of their own demise
from that treacherous campaign,

Make Spain Great Again!

in bloody field notes, in bullhorns
and sirens of ruin; in appendages of institutes
and technocratic amate grammar; in future bark
and shadow progenitors

in Pre-Columbian body cams
and closed-circuit storyboards
in classrooms, voluntold by friars
to tap the story, tap the story out.

interstitial: Yago S. Cura

The text (Florentine Codex) guides our work (and Sandy's work). It's a text that simultaneously records the history and destruction of the Mexica—we look to predict the history of our impact as children of the union of the Americas: (N America vs EEUU and L Americans vis a vis GringoYankees). This project is also important because of Operation Condor and the destabilization offered to the peace-loving people of Latin America by the efforts of the School of the Americas at Fort Benning, GA, a U.S. Army training facility, largely for Spanish-speaking Latin American cadets and officers. This project is a continuation of many of Eduardo Galeano's integral questions regarding the uneven relationship between N and S Americans developed in *Las Venas Abiertas de Latino America*, etc.

The themes of Justice, Immigration, Colonization, Borders, and of Codices spoke to me. The artists and writers spoke to me. The portraits of the Guatemalan children and the accompanying map spoke to me. All modern paintings made with Pre-Colombian pigment techniques speak to me, but figurative paintings rendered with the elements of the Florentine Codex are integral
    The pandemic affected my view of the project. The tlacuilos of the 16th century were making

interstitial: Yago S. Cura

a book for Sahagún while at the same time dealing with the physical challenges presented by pandemic living arrangements. For example, the tlacuilos were in the bowels of this colegio terribly busy making the *Historia General* while dealing with familial and interpersonal squabbles and still had to produce and make this encyclopedia of the way their lives used to be lived. Most importantly this project taught me how we can contribute to have a better future through thinking and creating jointly.

Quarantined Tongues

CONQUEST & RESISTANCE

Detail of *Calavera Copters* by Sandy Rodriguez, acrylic on plexiglass, Photo credit: J6 Creative. 2018. Collection of the artist

1532

Adrian Arancibia

"Llegando está el carnaval quebradeño, mi cholita
Erke, charango y bombo carnavalito para bailar..."

the pieces
left.
the pieces
left.
from the corners of my mouth.
singing the songs
left behind from another
place. another
era.

always,
earth, and hands, and space.
deeper. deeper. than puna.
deeper. deeper than inhales.
deeper. than afternoons in a plaza.
deeper. than children with zampoñas.
deeper. than lakitas
deeper. than kena breaths.
deeper. pachamama listening
to breaths.
to breaths.

the backbeat.
hitting the head
a child left to come
back.
eleven years
later, after the fall
of tenóchtitlan,
cuzco would fall
a shoulder of a condor.

and we come home
to breathe.
to moments

still reverberating.

always something
tugging heart
home. home, to a territorio
        to in between spaces.
home to a memory.
to a girl, that dances
bouncing cholulos.
at the edge of mountains.

learning the fight
before men
understood, weren't gods.
but men.
men.

call me aymara
call me chango
call me mapuche

"me preguntaron como vivia
me preguntaron,
sobreviviendo dije,
sobreviviendo."

survival never
just, the song
but the reto.
the virgins.
the curas.
the sacerdotes.
words made write
words made rite
words made right
on scrolls.

we find ways of taking out
from kekos
cholulos
pejesapos
guanacos

from tamarugal
to anemona.

in breath.
in breath.

24 Karat

Adolfo Guzman-Lopez

Gold on mulberry and fig fibers.
Gold is a footprint on the sloping lomas on the paper.

See the bird hold a drop,
it's a tear, una lagrima that'll drop into the word turned wave.

All other colors pale.
The blues you see come from the center of the earth,
on this painting they hit the Oaxaca coast as waves.

Gold is so little.
Gold was supposed to heal.
Gold rose like steam away from your hands.

The grandmothers stand on both sides,
the grandmothers heal
with water, with shields, a magen, a star.

The borders pulse
like the neon along Avenida Revolución in the 90s.

Gold is such a small part of what we have to give
and so much of what you want to take.

interstitial: Arminé Iknadossian

Today, right now, colonization, destruction, genocide is happening as I write this. The shame and reality of the inhumane treatment of refugees in the US border towns, apartheid in Israel, genocide in Myanmar, Armenia's sovereignty being threatened by Turkey and Azerbaijan, Black citizens being murdered by police in the USA, Indigeous women missing in large numbers, maquiladora workers being kidnapped and killed in Juarez.

We look back to the history of North and South America 500 years ago, and we see the same actions and motivations that drive imperialism today all over the world. Victimizing indigenous peoples, burning their sacred texts, trying to erase the Nahuatl language, making it illegal to write, paint, make medicine. As writers and artists, we must come together to destroy imperialist mindsets, white supremacy and colonialism. We come together to honor the artists and scribes who came before us, to light up their legacy in the dark room of ignorance.

Being unsilenced, speaking truth to power, giving back to the people who are from this land. These themes and actions are more important than ever.

I especially relate to Sandy's painting of the

mountains with shadows of a woman and child running, which represents the municipal yellow signs on the freeways near the Mexico/California border warning drivers to be careful. That image was seared into my memory from childhood, visiting San Diego, seeing those ominous signs, wondering why those families were fleeing, myself a political refugee from Lebanon. I did not understand back then that there were refugees everywhere.

    Diana and Sandy explained how the tlacuilos were also under pressure to produce texts while living through hardship. We live during a pandemic today, yet we continue to create. Creation is necessary to balance the scales.

mirror of your eyes unseen

gloria enedina alvarez

the cold hand's crystal silence colors the season... blank lips at a distance stretch unpronounced name... an ocean carried washes over... then breathes forgiveness from skin... erased like a fistful of dust...

Calaveracopteros

Yago S. Cura

hovering skulls and bones
over Veracruz and South LA
pero tinycitos, super pequeñcito
rotor guiro ratchet gnat partisanos
flip the cumbia switches, within
over the Mission and Hialeah
this centrifuge surface-to-air-history
in savage cavalry army mirage
speakers descend from the fuselage
over Spanish-Harlem and Pilsen
orange, bloated vapors of the sun's lucre
target acquisition Nativist traditions
mini-cumulonimbus chopper armada
over Roxbury and Watts and Logan barrio

The White Leather Bracelet

Darren J. de Leon

The white leather
        cuff bracelet appeared oddly strange
against my sienna
        skin.
As if my body
        was visiting privilege,
            until all
of my air
        exited through
your copper knee
        which was purposely
            firmly
        planted on
            my neck.

Tiles, Scans, and Strong Feet

Darren J. de Leon

Then, it started with an image of
freedom and boats carrying the oppressed.

Now, the leaves that heal our lungs
are capsuled and sweetened.

Then, the awakening of tired eyes
as hearts are drawn towards the shore.

Now, we walk through desert
gardens renamed as intrusive weeds.

Then, trekking, working, searching
for a sip of the new elixir called young country.

Now, the shimmering of the quetzal's tail
warns us of jeeps and infrared jails.

Then, broken mirrors and faded
pictures, scarves with the silent scent of the past.

Now, descriptions of a plague in burnt books
written for us to stray away from extinction.

Then, warm showers with bracero asylum,
their exits coated with dust bowl relief and DDT.

Now, in yerbas we trust,
in white tiled rooms we rust.

ANCESTOR BODIES

Detail of *Mapa de los Child Detention Centers and Family Separation and Other Atrocities* by Sandy Rodriguez. Photo credit: J6 Creative. Collection of the artist

new moon

gloria enedina alvarez

That's why we need to reach into the earth with our words coursing through our hands...so that they can return once more, new but old with the strength, the knowledge, the wisdom that is witness, purpose within action, within love, colors the vibrations, the music of time...face up...cara, corazón y manos...that's what the antigu@s would say, face, heart, and hands!

the body pulse

gloria enedina alvarez

the voice like sun in waking dreams not yet dreams wander not lost walking along

shadows stolen in the search beyond sealed heart ear over emptied chest hand

pressed to hear

interstitial: Darren J. de Leon

Growing up in the United States, one can obtain a historical education about this country, yet never understand the actual history of the land on which this country was founded. Project 1521 not only addresses the historical injustice of that miseducation, but also allows me as an indigenous Xicano to write about my relationship to the earth on which I stand.

The formal concept of immigration and the governing policies as defined by the occupying government were completely foreign to the indigineous societies that were nomadic, splintered or derivative of larger populations such as the Mejica. As a citizen of this country, I've come to accept the lineage of my bloodline that dates back many generations before Manifest Destiny and the Treaty of Guadalupe, both of which were intended to erase the trail of my personal cultural and biological history. When the U.S./Mexico border was established, I was involuntarily captured and detained through citizenship and the natural birth law established by the occupying government. My parents nor relatives completely understood these circumstances behind our existence other than the birth certificates which labelled me "white" and the late-night exchanges of personal stories of family history while in drunken states.

It is through my poetry that I can liberate myself, give myself a new name, manifest the type of life that I want to live. It is through poetry that I can reverse the thievery, death and injustice that has occurred to us once our world was transformed and colonized. It is through poetry that we can now begin to write the end of conquest and fill the world with healing, stories and love.

ENTRE Y CUANDO

gloria enedina alvarez

Y cuando dices
Es día
Despierta lugares
Donde anduve
Me devuelve mil pasos
Me levanta recorridos
Pues el día
Pone al corazón
A dividir el tiempo compartido
Porque el día
Eres tú
Tú voz
Conversación
Que suele ser
Una palabra sola

Between When at Times

gloria enedina alvarez

When you say
It is day
It awakens places
Where I've walked
It returns
A thousand steps
It lifts journeys
Well, the day
Makes the heart
Divide time shared
Because the day
Is you
Your voice
Conversation
 That seems to be
 One word alone

Julia Bogany on empowering the future

I think when our lives connect us
by our journeys that we're taking.
Right?
So, I had my grandma die...at 42, my mom died at 50.
So, when I turned 70, I decided, wait a minute,
I can't do this for my grandma no more,
they weren't here.
Right?
I have to do it for my grands and great-grands.
So, I had to change that.
Now I'm doing this with my great granddaughter,
cause I'm giving her the torch to go forward.
She's the one that's learning the language.
Right?
And, so she has to take that other path forward into the next generation.
Right?
And then that's how we pass things down and beyond.
We have to go...
So there's our generation that's looking for how our People *survived*
and *who they were*
and not just seeing them as nobody,
but as *really intelligent people.*
Right?
That...only we can tell the stories
and then we take it to the next generations
to *empower* the future.

Extracted from a conversation with Tongva Elder Julia Bogany on August 9, 2020.

TO BE VISIBLE

81

WRITER'S BIOS

gloria enedina alvarez embodies elegance and grace. her work examines life, in all its turbulence and glory. chicana poet, intermedia artist, playwright, librettist, translator, and curator, co-founder of many artists organizations, mentor to generations of artists, teaches creative writing, has won numerous awards, her poetry, librettos, and plays have been published and performed in us, latin america, and europe. publications include emerging en un mar de olanes, la excusa/the excuse, poetry collections jn english and spanish, and spoken word cd, centerground, along with anthologies and periodicals.

A San Diego professor and author, **Adrián Arancibia** was born in Iquique, Chile. A cofounder of the Taco Shop Poets and editor the *Taco Shop Poets Anthology: Chorizo Tonguefire*, he is the author of three collections of poetry, the latest of which is a collection titled *Poems of Exhaustion*. Arancibia holds a Ph.D. in Comparative Literature and is a professor of English and Creative Writing at Miramar College.

Julia Bogany (1948-2021) served as Cultural Ambassador of the Gabrieleno-Tongva Tribe. She helped to reawaken and revive Tongva language, arts, and culture through teaching classes and workshops in community settings, colleges, universities, and k-12 schools. Ms. Bogany worked for over thirty years for the American Indian community, providing cultural, FASD, and ICWA trainings throughout California. She served as a community health worker for California Indian Education Association and member of the California Native American College Board. Ms. Bogany was active in the Children Court L.A. Round Table, ran co-ed and women's circles, and consulted with teachers and school boards on how to revise curriculum to reflect an accurate history of California Tribes.

Yago S. Cura is an Adult Services Librarian for the LAPL @ the Miriam Matthews-Hyde Park Branch. He runs HINCHAS de Poesía Press (www.hinchaspress.com) and makes zines with his oldest son, and writes poems in his spare time, which is never, so don't ask.

Yago publishes *Librarians with Spines* (www.librarianswithspines.com) series with Max Macias and Autumn Anglin, *Inspiring Library Stories* with Oleg Kagan, and *X LA Poets* with Linda Ravenswood.

Darren J. de Leon is an award-winning poet from San Bernardino. He earned his Masters Degree in English from San Francisco State University and has published poetry in numerous publications including the University of Arizona Press, Cipactli, and Fourteen Hills. In 1996, he founded Los Delicados: Poetas del Sol, San Francisco's avant garde leaders of the Latino Spoken Word scene.

Adolfo Guzman-Lopez. There is a photo of Adolfo, less than one year old, in his father's arms, his mother looking on, at El Cerro del Tepeyac. There's a photo of Adolfo at seven years-old wearing a Wayne Newton collar, with the Tlatelolco colonial church, the pre-Columbian ruins, and a 1960s modernist building in the background. There's a photo of Adolfo reading poetry at a Roberto's taco shop. There's a photo of Adolfo interviewing Frank Gehry. There's a blurry photo of Adolfo dancing in the Prado Ballroom with his beautiful bride. There's a photo of Adolfo with a bloody wound at the bottom of his neck from a foam round fired by police during the George Floyd protests. There will be photos of Adolfo loving his daughter and his son. For everything else: Google-it!

Sara Harris is a sound artist, Master Gardener, and journalist with more than 20 years of experience in Los Angeles, Mexico, and the Netherlands. She has produced award-winning work for Youth Radio, Marketplace, and hosted/produced *Hear in the City* (Pacifica Foundation). Sound installations include *Oficios de la Calle* at Museo de las Culturas Populares in Mexico City, and *Regeneración: Three Generations of Revolutionary Ideology*, at the Vincent Price Art Museum in L.A. Current projects include experimental documentary *The Fragmentations Only Mean* (2022) with Jesse Lerner.

Arminé Iknadossian was born in Beirut, Lebanon and immigrated to the United States in 1974 to escape the civil war. She is the author of *All That Wasted Fruit* (Main Street Rag Press), a collection of poems about the sacred feminine. She earned her MFA from Antioch University. Armine teaches high school English and serves on the advisory board of IALA (International Armenian Literary Association) where she mentors emerging poets. She also teaches creative writing online for Surprise the Line. She has received fellowships from Idyllwild Arts, The Los Angeles Writing Project and Anaphora Arts.

Diana Magaloni is a renowned art historian, author and conservator. She is currently the Deputy Director, Program Director, and Virginia Fields Curator of the Art of the Ancient Americas at the Los Angeles County Museum of Art. She was formerly the Director of the Museo Nacional de Antropología in Mexico City (2009-2013). Her book *'Colors of the New World: Materials, Artists, and the Creation of the Florentine Codex'* (2014) was reviewed as a book that opens new ways of understanding art.

Linda Ravenswood de Montaño (BFA, MA, PhD abd) is a poet and performance artist from Los Angeles. A co-founding member of Melrose Poetry Bureau, and founder and editor-in-chief of The Los Angeles Press (www.thelosangelespress.com), Linda's recent publications include *XLA POETS*, and *rock waves / sloe drags* (Eyewear London, 2021). Be in touch @TheLosAngelesPress

Sandy Rodriguez is a Los Angeles-based artist. Her work investigates the methods and materials of painting across cultures and histories. Her *Codex Rodriguez-Mondragón* is made up of a collection of maps and paintings about the intersections of history, social memory, contemporary politics, and cultural production. Most recently she has been awarded the Caltech-Huntington Art + Research Residency and a Creative Capital Award for 2021.

ACKNOWLEDGEMENTS

The poets of Project 1521 are grateful for the generous gifts and donations to our fundraising campaign. Without their support this book would have not been possible. We thank the following: Jennifer Josten, Barbara Osborn, Diana Magaloni, John Rabe, Karina Hodoyan, Guzman-Lopez Family, Yago S. Cura, Sandy Rodriguez, Lydia Pinto-Nguyen, Ernestina Osorio, Cynthia Briano, John Gonzalez, Claudia Quintana, Tina Demirdjian, Lorena Villegas, Kim Abeles, Paul S. Flores, Kitty Felde Daley, Joyce J. Lu, Sharah Nieto, Laurel Ann Bogen, Martin A. Blasco, Nancy Bulacio, Arminé Iknadossian, David Herrera, Adriana Zavala, Annabeth Headrick, Florencia Bazzano, Susanna Esquivias Nikkhou, Shannah Rose, Camille Taiara, Josiah Luis Alderete, David McIntire, Susan Hayden, John Gonzalez, George Sanchez, Annabeth Headrick, Adriana Zavala, Kim Richter, Tatiana Reinoza, and 8 anonymous donors.

ABOUT PROJECT 1521

Project 1521 is a cadre of poets, scholars, and an artist generating literary and visual works as acts of resistance. *"Tlacuilx: Tongues in Quarantine"* is the first volume of poetry created by the members of this group. This volume is published by Los Angeles-based independent Hinchas de Poesía Press.

The collaboration began between L.A. based artist Sandy Rodriguez and writer poet/journalist Adolfo Guzman-Lopez and was inspired by Indigenous perspectives on the Spanish invasion and the 500 years since the fall of the Aztec Empire in 1521.

The group has performed works at the Pasadena LitFest, Beyond Baroque in 2019, the exhibition titled *You Will Not Be Forgotten* at the Charlie James Gallery, and the *Tongues In Quarantine Virtual Poetry Brunch*.

A ten part series entitled, "*Project 1521 Podcast*" was produced by Darren J. de Leon, Adolfo Guzman-Lopez, and Sara Harris. The episodes feature interviews, live recordings, discussions, and original poetry from members of Project 1521. The podcast will give you an insight into the work of modern day Tlaquilos and the publication of their work. You can hear the series through the QR code below or where your favorite podcasts can be heard.

ISBN: 978-1-954640-03-0

Look for
TLACUILX: TONGUES IN QUARANTINE E-book
from
Hinchas de Poesia Press

E-BOOK

More from Hinchas de Poesia Press

Librarians with Spines, Vol. 01
edited by Max Macias and Yago Cura (2017)
ISBN: 978-0-9845398-8-8

Librarians with Spines, Vol. 02
edited by Max Macias and Yago Cura (2018)
ISBN: 978-1-7324848-2-5

XLA Poets
edited by Linda Ravenswood
ISBN: 978-1-73244848-3-2

Inspiring Library Stories: Tales of Kindness, Connection, and Community Impact
edited with essays, by Oleg Kagan
ISBN: 978-1-7324848-6-3

Zine Subscriptions

The James Foley Scriptorium

www.HINCHAspress.com
Instagram @hinchas_press

www.ingramcontent.com/pod-product-compliance
Lightning Source LLC
Chambersburg PA
CBHW021430070526
44577CB00001B/142